With A Certain Wide-Eyed Look

Doug Hodges

For SoloSpeak,
my shining star of Texas,
who led me home

authorHOUSE®

AuthorHouse™
1663 Liberty Drive
Bloomington, IN 47403
www.authorhouse.com
Phone: 1-800-839-8640

Unless otherwise noted, all works, herein, are the author's. Any 'worked' images were accomplished with Adobe Photoshop Elements 9.

Published by AuthorHouse 11/15/2013

ISBN: 978-1-4918-3407-7 (sc)
ISBN: 978-1-4918-3408-4 (e)

Library of Congress Control Number: 2013920710

This book is dedicated to
Joan Juskie,
fellow poet.
Who, perhaps more than anyone else,
our links and chains,
have helped me to
honor the past
and embrace the future.

Contents

Prologue

for a poet
there is no greater joy
than experiencing.
life is from whence
come words.
I have always been alert, attentive
wide-eyed and awestruck with the world
around me -
people, places, incidents...
if memory serves,
I wrote my first poem
in the fifth grade
and have never ceased.
I do not think myself
overly prolific,
yet often wonder at the sheer volume
a lifetime can turn out;
this, despite the words lost
to time and changes,
purges and happenstance.
interestingly enough,
those images recorded in my mind
remain... though sometimes
tinted by newer ones
... and the words come out,
when they are ready.
a poet does not look for an audience...

he or she is the audience;
yet, we are overcome with
joy and amazement when
an audience does develop...
for which we humbly give thanks
to God and man.
poets can be craftsmen
yet, we are not formed
like journalists and tellers of tales.
we, like unwritten music,
waft on the wind until our time
is come.
Doug Hodges 7/26/13

Shrimp boat, <u>Captain Cheito</u>,
Port of Brownsville, Texas - 2003

Morning

the morning was filled with
the smell of fish
shrimp boats made their way
inland through the channel
in the distance a cane field
was burning
black and pungent smoke
filled the air like
low-lying clouds

11/5/99

El Rio Bravo

El Rio Bravo
sparkles in the morning sun
like it was cloaked in diamonds
as it meanders its way to the sea.
the banks rise on either side
tiny escarpments topped
with grass and cacti.
on the southern shore
graze a horse and a cow
oblivious of the muddy
slow-moving river
that has known such turmoil

11/3/99

Por mi amor

there is no color to love.
love is a penetrating light,
bright and all-encompassing,
starting from deep within,
it fills one's soul, one's heart,
so fully spreading throughout the body
that love radiates,
through love's smile,
love's depthless eyes,
the magic in love's voice,
the electric loving touch of the fingers,
love's very step with its rhythm and song.
love spreads from one to two
and beyond, touching the world
transcending space and time
and this singular dimension we call reality.

12/13/99

I

I want to flow like water
to sing the word
to dance like leaves in the wind
to not think or feel
anything but existence and life
I would rather fly in the
teeth of the greatest storm, unfettered
than to be chained in a golden palace

1/11/00

You

you never know how far you can go until you try
you never know how far you can go to hell and
God's mountaintop to rocky peaks of ecstasy
and deserts of despair, wastelands of
city-minded refuse yearning to breathe free...
you never know when birds sing life and
trains snort death and rabbits may indeed have
more spirituality than we credit ourselves
with civilizations of Babbling towers lost in decaying and
impenetrable jungles of our conceit...
you never know when light will dawn piercing the fog of
long-forgotten transgressions which wall us into
keeps we have not named...
the light is our focus, flowers our children and
legacy like fog spreads before us
dissipating with each breath.

　　　10/7/00

Words

words that will come
will come, unbidden;
dark thoughts
on a happy day,
strange and disjointed
unsettling and disturbing.
yet they are as the blood
in my veins
on their way to be cleansed.
I must acknowledge them
like a tip of my hat
to a stranger
and let them go

   11/14/00

Vida Bravo

My life winds like a river
Indeed, there are moments
When it is choked with plant life
And lies turgid, faltering
Even occasionally halted
By whatever sand bar
Sea and hurricane wind
May throw up

My path has changed
Twisting this way and that
Reforming the borders of
An ever-changing map
Yet, I flow on,
Undaunted on my course
Whether waters be trapped, diverted
Or free as the wild desert
Through times of flood and drought
I am

5/14/01

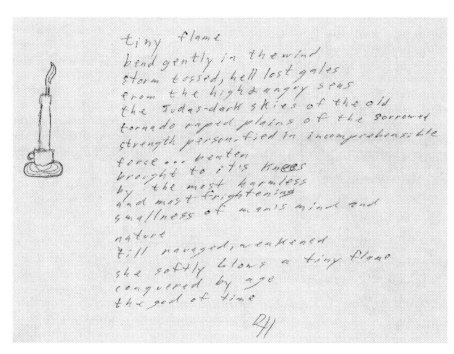

tiny flame
bend gently in the wind
storm tossed, hell lost gales
from the high & angry seas
the Judas-dark skies of the old
tornado raped plains of the sorrowed
strength personified in incomprehensible
force... beaten
brought to it's knees
by the most harmless
and most frightening
smallness of a ems mind and

nature
till ravaged, weakened
she softly blows a tiny flame
conquered by age
the god of time

- From my unpublished
volume of illustrated poems,
<u>The Face Poems</u>

From my unpublished volume:
The Face Poems

How 'fantastique'

how fantastique
to knit up the raveled sleeve
of time
while bleeding softly
in the rhyme
we call our shepherds
from afar
gently snoring
at the bar

     6/75

To think is to fly

to think is to fly
to fly is to be free
we are haunted
by the freedom
deep within
our souls
struggling
to be
released

     6/75

And we say

and we say
"How are you"
to the empty
theatre
and nod and
wink our eye.
for empty seats
do not laugh
but neither
do they
lie.

7/21/81

I have flown with hawks

I have flown with hawks and sparrows
my brother is the wild goose
I have held
all the birds
within my
breast
but I turned
the eagle
loose

7/21/81

Clouds

clouds
roll through the mountains
filling the valleys
and flying across the peaks
cloaking time
and space
creating a here-ness
a comforting "now"
that wears like
an old coat

   2/17/95

Face upon the

face upon the plane of time
lost betwixt
myself and thine
are you a shade
some warning sign
or is the face you wear
truly mine?

   2/17/95

Mr. Grump says:

Mr. Grump says:
They are all liars.
Why do you think
we put them in political office?
So they would all be in one
place.

2/17/95

Mr. Moon

Mr. Moon,
who is full
of himself tonight,
says:
Anyone can live.
It is dying that is
an art.

2/17/95

A travesty lightly taken

someone upon
sometime I seemed
to have seen
somewho
somewhere
somewhen

were that I could be
that which I had been

or perhaps,
were that I could be
that somewho
whom I had seen
someonce upon
sometime

somewhere around the millennium

There are few enough of us left who remember the hot, cloying smell of melting lead; of how the very air would permeate your clothes in smell and even color; of the constant clanging and buzzing and clinking of 'make up' in the old days of hot-medal printing. To those that don't... most present-day readers... once upon a time, a large, heavy weight of lead would be suspended on a hook over a melting pot into which the lead would slowly be lowered. The melted lead would flow into trays where it would immediately start to cool and while cooling an image (in reverse to our eyesight) would be stamped upon it by a man sitting at a keyboard, not unlike that of a typewriter. When enough characters to fill a single line of type (newspaper or book column) the line would be shuttled into a tray where all the lines would stack until the tray was filled. Then this tray would be emptied onto a rolling metal table called a 'Turtle' where it would be added to many other columns of type and/or art mattes (for photos and illustrations). The whole page would be fitted together like a jig-saw puzzle and clamped down tight and taken to a machine which would create a paper-mache matte. From this, a metal plate would be made which would then be put onto the printing press. Very briefly, this was the world of hot-metal.

Electronics brought so many drastic changes, so fast, that a mere twenty years replaced several hundred in the publication of printed communication. As always, this transition period period was traumatic, both invigorating and fatal.

I wrote the following poem somewhen back in those dim days and was honored to have it published in the Boulder Daily Camera's house newspaper, 'Eye of the Camera' in the Spring 1990 (vol. IX, #2) issue.

A Day at the Newspaper

The clang, clang, clickety-clack, choingg
of the linotype machine
has long since given way
to the beep, peowp, whirr
of the headache-causing fluorescent eye
of the electronic terminal.
Where once an entire line of type had to be re-typed
to correct an error,
now the slightest touch of a single finger
can eliminate an individual character,
a sentence, a paragraph, and even, God help us,
the entire article.
Where once there was grace given
to the unaccomplished novice,
now only swift and
unhesitating retribution
remain.

Once man was master of the machine;
repairs were made with sweat, thought,
paper clips and chewing gum.
Now required is an electronic operating room
with tedious and complicated maneuvers
rivaling those on General Hospital...
although a swift fist to the top
ofa recalcitrant machine still seems to work miracles.
Once type was limited to size, height and width;
each font was distinctive and proud;
now any font can become any other
through the miracle of modern electronic manipulation;

width and depth, even italics, can be
rendered unrecognizable.
Now it is truly possible to put ten pounds of it
into a five pound bag.

And late at night
when the tube glares out at me mockingly
seemingly daring me to find something better
my mind flickers back
to the noisy but comforting,
plodding but effective,
hot and greasy-smelling days of hot metal
and I wonder if the chaotic sterility,
the electronic domination,
the emasculating wizardry of the now
might not be dangerous.
Maybe, it is the lack of control
the knowing that you are in
speedy and shocking hands and
that when the power goes off
you are truly in the dark.

Spring 1990

From Songs of Colorado:
Ramblings on Denver

Denver squats like a giant wart
on the high plains,
half old - half new.
a monumental example of man's
time, greed and
natural state of confusion.
she is elegant in her
architectural history,
and glorious in her
cast-concrete monolithic present.
she is lost in the half-finished state
of her highways to the future.
the mountains to her west
rise proud and white.
sometimes, there is a cloud of pollution
opaquing their image.
as if seen through murky waters,
less common now...
proof that some problems
do get worked out.
likewise, the downtown area
has been prettied up into a mall,
with bright funky shops
and a free bus running up and down;
a far cry from the filthy and dingy refuse
which it had been not too long ago.
I wonder where that refuse went?
she is a city trying hard to prove herself
in a world of cities.
a small gathering place that long ago
outgrew its smallness.

1985

Boulder

she was shorter than five foot
sitting upon an upturned box,
legs casually crossed,
playing her guitar;
a much patched and beat-up case
lay open before her
holding a sign which read,
"Support Boulder's Women Artists".
her long hair flowed
unkempt and dirty
in the wild Boulder wind,
dancing with the music.
her face wasn't pretty, nor plain;
large and chiseled,
older than it should have been.
her jeans were well worn, relatively clean,
covered with the patches of necessity.
on her feet were dark, heavy, slip-on shoes.
her fingers made the music,
which graced the mountains,
who returned it in the blowing wind.
she sang rarely and when she did,
the voice was soft and ragged,
range-less, and as worn as her jeans.

1995

The Crystal Club
Crystal City, Colorado - 1980s
*Photograph by the author and previously published
with my column: 'The Trail's End' - Gazette Telegraph 10/6/84.*

Colorado Ghosts

warped and weathered boards,
old before any of us were born,
still stand defiantly in the face of time;
huddling, as if from the wind,
in a secluded mountain canyon.
the streets are non-existent
and the structures appear
to have been erected haphazardly.

a ghostly music
echoes in the chilly air,
a badly out of tune 'pianer'
tinnily pounds out
old favorites, no longer remembered.
the music drifts out from the saloon,
branded as such by the wide doorway,
now choked with brush.
a large rectangular sign tilts above the step.
what it could have said is anyone's guess
but for sure, it was enough to bring in those
seeking refreshment and entertainment;
miners, ranchers, and anyone else
lucky or unlucky enough to find themselves
stuck in such a place, at such a time.

in winter, the entrance
would have to be constantly dug out
from the continuously falling snow
and, for a place of this size,
there must have been at least two cast iron stoves

lending a black pall to a place
already pungent with the smoke from
pipes, cigars, 'brain tablets', oil lamps and
God knows what...
the noise would be amplified
by the closed doors; a noise so loud
as to deafen one under normal circumstances...
competing with the constant roar of voices
would be the plunking of bottles on bar and table,
the sliding of coins, the slapping of cards,
the bouncing of dice, the whooshing of a 'lucifer'
as it was struck to light the cigar of a man
trying not to let on that he had drawn
to an inside straight... and lost.

when space provided, there would be
dancing, the sound of tapping and stomping feet,
the swishing of clothing; the creak of leather,
coats and chaps, holsters, gloves and hats...
as thick as the smoke are the cloying scents -
the stench of cheap whiskey, stale beer, sweat
and vomit; the stink of horse, mule and
other livestock mixed with tobacco and perfume.
even now, the barren and decaying walls
radiate the smells and still show the scars of smoke.

a ruined staircase, impossibly dangerous,
leading to mysterious rooms above,
sits like a monolithic skeleton.
broken furniture lies about, in careless abandon.
paintings, mirrors, brass rails, spittoons,
glassware and bottles are long gone.
an occasional beer or whiskey bottle may yet be found,
but of a must later vintage,
possibly left by one of those very souls

who walked off with an original.
the floor is warped and lumpy from time,
weather, and a thousand feet.
bullet holes can still be found
if one takes the time to seek them out.
the music now seems to be playing a sad old cowboy tune.

I am careful of the rotten steps as I walk
back into the cold wind of the mountain fall.

1984

Revisiting 1999:
Denver Homage

the temples of man
rise unto the Lord
and shine golden
in the morning sun.
to the west
rise other temples
white-capped peaks
stretching upward,
also golden with the sun.
the temples of man
reach for heaven
in praise and prayer;
the mountains quietly
rise up and
become one with heaven.

5/13/99

I followed a Spanish Star to the Texas coast...

we watched the Dolphin dance
male and female
they love and play
call each other by name
and sing their praises
to creation.
they do not fight
they do not make war
they do not take
without giving.
in their custody,
the sea is safe and secure.
we would be Dolphin
of the land,
you and I

5/13/99

The Sylvia Beach Hotel is a Bed and Breakfast
hanging off the Oregon coast. Each room bears the
theme of a different author.
The dinner games are lively.

Re: Sylvia Beach Hotel

our shelters are made
of need and comfort.
here is a nook
of space and time,
of authors and words.
a large old wooden building
on a cliff
overlooking the
endlessly sounding sea.
those who pass through,
lend their own words,
intermingling their lives,
briefly and in a small way,
with these authors,
in whose room they stay;
rooms that time-slip
the mind
and tickle the imagination

5/21/99

The Tap-dancer

he came dancing
dancing
smiling and tapping
weaving and bowing
we thought we knew
him then
as he laughed and
made us one
with his
dancing joy

time moves on
and minds and bodies change
and the tap-dancer died
yet, in the back of our
minds and our hearts
and our very spirits
he dances there still
in frivolous gaiety
making us one
with his
dancing joy

for Dale
7/4/76

I do like candles

I do like candles
the flames
so fragile
so deadly
as they gently flicker
with an unfelt breeze
the colors flowing in and out

sometimes the wax
flows down
creating bizarre sculptures
here - massive and dull
here - intricate, entwining
sometimes fat candles
become hollow
with the light moving
as if behind isinglass

the smell is of warmth
and is comforting

- Rollinsville 1990

Rock of Ages
- The Great American Southwest

Ripples in a coffee cup...

there are times when the blahhs
come in, not on cat feet
but as an iron curtain...
I am oppressed
yet, never overwhelmed.
I but need a moment's respite
to catch my breath
and sing my song...
a flash back to a clear chilly mountain-top
or hand-in-hand along a golden southern beach
a green meadow lush with wild raspberries
an ivory rock as mammoth as a whale...
seagulls or ravens, armadillo or moose
the sky is my sky
the stars are my stars
and...
I am renewed
as intended

     5/13/13

To Brenda - RIP

time there was... and was again
when the mountains were as young as eternity
and love was but a green stem
as flexible and unyielding as the universe
flowing not as a river
but rather many streams
over, across, under and around
the pitfalls and misunderstandings
of a jaded world
when campfires were storybooks
opening incredible and mysterious vistas
not half as scary as the world around us

we came naked and new into such wind
which blew us hither and yon
and beyond all comprehension
lakes of wine, frigid in the mountain air
baptized us into other realms
tried to shield us from the violence and chaos
of green jungles, swamps and senseless abandon
from parents and governments that should have known
better... even unto mind expansion and
wanton experimentation were we all still captives
of our shriven souls while God listened on
one hand applauding in the empty theatre

     with love
     1/20/2012

Marcy Reed

another funeral
they seem to come so often, now
during the funeral service
her white casket open
Marcy looks calm and at peace
surreal upon a cloud
nothing at all like I knew her
the spark of her smile has gone
I wonder if her colorful
fuzzy slippers reside within
the words drone on
I can see her soul
become a butterfly
golden against the cloudy white
and up she goes
fly, Marcy, fly

February 27, 2012

In Silence

in silence walk I along
not even sound of bird nor wind
can enter my self-erected cocoon
I choose to be withdrawn
unto myself, answerable to no one
I am the proverbial Paul Simon 'Rock'

yet, I have not entombed myself for fear of hurt
nor have I chosen to flee an arduous life
I walk along, here, merely to wonder
to think within myself
shunning man and God alike
it is my quiet time, a self-imposed time out

all too soon, God returns
along with the greeting of the birds
the gentle tugging of the wind
welcoming me back to a world
in which I know I have a place
like an over-exerted engine,
I just needed a rest

poem chain 4/11/12

Retired Life

retired life is an anomaly to me.
perhaps, if I ever actually receive money
for a life of leisure, that might change...
but then, what is a life of leisure?
I started out, a callow youth,
working lawns to buy my first car
through college and the army
I worked any number of curious jobs
shoveling salt, driving a cab
loading and unloading boxcars
delivering furniture, sweeping caves
... like some sort of bizarre 8mm home movie
it rolls through my mind.
I then drifted into my career in communication,
if career it may be called,
the newspapers, where I performed
any number of functions
and learned a great deal
about a technology that is now all but dead
about presses and cameras, computers and radios...
like my stint with the army,
all a vain attempt to learn something before
progress makes it obsolete
now, at 62, I go on.
there is always something to do,
always a horizon.
I work for no one but me and mine
yet my days are as busy as they ever were
with an employer.
perhaps, I no longer have a regular schedule,

a tracked frame, a point A to point B...
yet, I never did well with that at any age.
God abhors a vacuum and my glass
always fills no matter how fast
I may try to empty it

poetry chain 6/5/12

A Prayer this Sunday for old Colorado

the devastating fires
of summer...
hardly a moment to rest...
now, the Aurora shooting
to an area never recovered from
the Columbine shooting.
for, where time may make us hurt less,
may desensitize us
to a place where we can put an incident
on the back burner
proceed to go on with our lives,
the memory... the living of the tragedy
always remains
just waiting for some similar incident
to tear open the wound.
and, we all have so many wounds
whether local or national
or global
personal or
shared simply within the family of man.

we can offer little to the the participants of such tragedy
to the perpetrator or the victim
only our heartfelt empathy
a shoulder and a prayer
... for peace to those journeying on
for peace to those left behind
for peace to all those left to pick up
the pieces of shattered existence.
God, in his mysterious mercy,
has shown us at least two things:
the fragility of life
and the strength found therein.

7/22/12

Doppelgänger

there is a curiosity about myself...
on the one hand, there is "I"
the person I believe myself to be
un-aging... *relatively*...
easy-going... going with the flow
casting my pebbles into the pond
sending out gentle ripples of love and peace...

I look into the mirror, however
and there is a stranger
older, heavier, with thinning hair...
the blue eyes appear haunted
and an anger bubbles up from within
clenching hands into fists, grinding teeth;
this is the 'wolf' at my door.

I usually travel gaily along,
a smile ever on my face
a polite nod, a kind word
every ready to assist
full of the joy of every day
brimming with love towards my fellow man
a strong shoulder, a comforting hand...

then, a politician will smilingly cut
the throat of a nation,
some driver on a cell phone runs a red light,
a drunk piles up on the highway
killing all involved except himself,
even the weather being too hot
and oppressive;

worse, the lack of direction and purpose will raise its head
and I am embroiled in frustration,
anger has cut me apart
from my blessed normal world
and I am lost.

September 2012

Long-horn Armadillo
Houston, 2012

A Dream of Name

when I undid the first letter of my name
it is a 'D'
once upon a time it might have been a 'J'
the sands of my soul poured out
fine grains settled and piled about
the base of the letters
growing and flowing as dunes,
reaching higher and higher
until my name was awash,
looking engulfed and forlorn
like barren rocks in the midst
of some wind-swept desert
the sand never stopped,
though was unable to completely
obliterate the name altogether
there were the pillars of the 'H'
the domes of the first and middle 'Ds'
lumps denoting other more mysterious letters
the sand continued to pour out and about
and the desert grew until
the whole scene was consumed
it pours there still
in the wasteland of my mind
my soul consuming... protecting
yet, not consuming... nurturing
flowing like a khaki sea
comforting and shielding
loving and strengthening
isolating and erasing
a mere name

> *Douglas Dean Hodges*
> *9/14/12*

Jennie, Bernie, mothers and sons...

life is such a tapestry of layers
smaller lives within the greater scheme
old and new... i look back
and can not even remember
the one so young, who
trod the boards and plains
of the early "movin' on"
the tests and temptations of youth
the insecure excitement of it all
the indescribable glory of success,
the unendurable depthless-ness of failure and loss

i can barely touch that first love
the poignancy, the pain still remain
but faces are fuzzy, facts elusive
a first marriage... another... and on... and on
each as unique as a hand-tooled leather saddle
as new, soft, sleek and beautiful
... and what of those human beings
who are no longer a part of my world
do they not exist? like the existentialist's
falling tree in the forest
if no one is there to hear or see it,
does it makes no difference?
of course, that is not right!
human beings go on with their lives, marry others,
and have children who have their own children
and pour out their own ripples into the world
i may even meet some of these ripples on distant shores
without even knowing... or, perhaps knowing,

am so amazed as to be struck dumb.
egoist that i am, existentialist that i inherently am,
i do realize and understand the sanctity
and value of every human life.

i have spent my life communicating
and teaching, helping others to communicate
for that is what we are... our stories
our knowledge... that is what we share and leave
that, which makes us threads into the life-tapestries of others
for good or bad, we are there
and they, those others, are here within our own... forever

    9/28/12

Soliloquy on Freedom

when I was young
I misunderstood 'free choice'
I wanted to be free... I needed to be free
free from authority
be it parent, government, religion...
I had to make 'my' way
and I had to do it 'my way'
I survived the callowness of youth

along the way, I touched some people
and was, in turn, touched by others
I made and lost innumerable
bonds of friendship
and of love

I truly learned that there are consequences
consequences to each action
freely taken or not
and if I was to be held account
I decided it would be for actions
of my own choice

like Don Quixote
I tilted with my own windmills
neither winning nor losing
a non-existent war
yet, like America, herself,
there was always a war
one or the other in a eternal cycle
of open-ended struggle
until one day...

I heard the voice
tell me that it was 'I'
it was always 'I' who was reacting
the conceit of 'I'
that 'I' could ever change anything
that 'I' was mighty enough to stop
the hurricane
the flood
the fire

the voice told me that I was
just a part of the whole
a mere thread in a great tapestry
that any importance 'I' may have
lay in my ability to be a part
to do my part
to share and spread the wealth
of the gifts which 'I' had been given
not which 'I' had earned or created
for, indeed, 'I' had not

I had always been free
for freedom lay in my mind, my heart
and my soul
the only power the world takes over us
takes from us
is that which we choose to give
all the martyrs have taught us that
regardless of religion, sect or sex
truly, truly
"there is none so blind
as he who will not see"

10/11/12

Possessions

oh, I have possessions
with which I have been truly blessed
they surround me like a womb
giving me security and comfort
in fact, I am not, never have been, could never be
one of those with bare or even semi-bare walls and shelves
mine call out to me as old friends
fellow travelers
even alone in the forest, strange pieces of wood
interesting rocks, bone or bits of fur
would find their way to my campsite
however, that said, when life moves on
my possessions may, and do, come and go
to new homes, new friends
I learned that I can purge, if called upon
and neither I nor those possessions suffer for it

I have found that I can fill a tiny single room shack
or a mighty multi-roomed house
my possessions are a part of me, and I of them,
but we are not each other
what I truly am, is a conglomerate of all those beings
with which I have been blessed
which God had placed along my way
men, women, children and animals
the living essence of my path
all who have woven their lives into my own,
accepting part of mine into theirs
all the experiences, all the emotion
perceived good or ill... these are my threads

... and God, the true possessor
the true possession with which we are all blessed
that is I, the me

all the possession that I can need or want
is the love of God
filtered through the love of man and animal
the love that bonds man and woman into traveling mates
into parents blessing the earth with new life
love is a possession which possesses us
rather than the other way around

10/27/12

The Chill

in the slight chill of pre-fall
deer move silently through the chaparral
approaching one of the few waterholes
they look to the birds to warn them of danger
yet, the birds sing merrily
and flitter here and there as is their wont

while drinking, silence suddenly falls
instantaneously, the birds are squawking
the branches and brush move with their wings as if alive
something is on the move
something sleek and dangerous
the deer are gone

the cat is not large but sleek and shiny
yellow and brown mottled
she moves across the brush silently
oozing like a snake
pity the prey who heed not their surroundings
for she is hungry and merciless
culling the weary and unwary

poetry chain 10/5/12

Schemes

colorful splendor spreads out around me
be it the cactus flowers of the Rio Grande Valley
or the lush and cool rainforest of the great northwest
or the amazing wheat and corn fields of middle America
stretching in all directions as far as the eye can see
or on the lofty snow-topped peaks of purple mountains
majesty
it is a true blessing I have always acknowledge
always given thanks for
which never ceases to amaze me

despite man's depredations in the smaller scheme,
God's, in the larger, ever goes on.
the machinations of fortune,
for good or ill,
are viewed so by man
in how whatever affects him.
in our selfishness,
we fail to see that the test
is not in what happens but in how
man will react.
our glory lies in our actions.
we have no control over the moving finger of God,
nor should we.
our harmony with our God
lies in being a part of Him
allowing Him to be a part of us,
in going with the flow and being a part of that flow.

in green fields
I once lay down
watching clouds form into shapes
I saw a horse, a dog, a clown
even a hero, once, with flapping cape
as I gazed upon a face of God

and God, he smiled down at me
I began to wonder, to understand
in that moment, I began to see
all that had been given
all the possibilities

poetry chain 11/13/12

The Children of Sandy Hook

the words have all been said
the songs have all been sung
tragedy has wrung out all the tears

12/14/12

Solstice

I open up my heart
I open up my soul
I open up my arms
to all the children
of all ages
of all times and places
for we have only ourselves to share
to touch and be touched
quickly before moving on

as with God
as with the earth
I am an integral part
no less than a hurricane
no greater than a speck of dust
a spiritual link to the love
which bonds all
and...
I do humbly pray every new morning
with every sight
with every breath
that I am grateful
not because I am great
not because I have
but merely because
I am

Solstice 2012

Epiphany

so...
it came clear as a bell during Israel's sermon
after the quest... my transformation
God filled me with life
with Himself
to the point of bursting
where I was excited to let everyone know
to tell my story... hear the stories given to me
sing the songs
... and, as I traveled,
the flow kept coming
and I kept sharing as best I could

now, the ensuing years
I think, especially, the Christian aspect
(shades of the past, shades of my youth)
have slowly shut me off
not that God is no longer sending...
I have just stopped receiving
it started with the music... then the words... then the stories
even when I have heard or seen faint glimpses
I seemed unable to record them

thus, I sit
I am so very blessed... and so very happy
yet... what about the Spirits
am I done? is there to be no more?
is it truly as Israel speaks about the Bible...
That's all there is!
There will not, can not, be any more!

the age of miracles is past...
of direct communication with God
if the present age is of such 'reality',
that mystery can only be found in a book
(albeit, The Book of God),
what does that say to us? about us? about the 'now'?
is God truly finished!
is God done with me?
if my life has been a miracle, in an age without miracles,
how can that be over?
have I lost my willpower, my strength?
I was in tune... harmony flowed...
perhaps I got old?
yet, how can age have anything to do with anything
considering the age of all the patriarchs of all the faiths
God speaks to all who will... and apparently who can, listen

I feel as I did when I was a child
I had the Church on one hand... I had God on the other
one was a duty, a pattern to my life
a bulwark, a staple
the other was the very breath of life
the air, the earth, all the creatures thereof
were a part of me... as I was of them
God dwelt within me and I within Him
yet, I could never bring the two together
the wrong words kept the two worlds apart
yet, I had to live in both
and could never be wholly of either
... a long time passed where I was of neither
life took me on a strange twisting journey of its own
where I was torn asunder and reshaped
shaman-like, I was refashioned into
someone who could speak
yet, I had nothing to say

until Raven came
and life unfolded anew, like petals of a flower
and Raven and Coyote, all the Spirits
the Great Spirit, Himself, filled me
and I was flying... alive and aloft

1/18/13

A-pondering

treat myself well, I do
often enough, at least.
sometimes I wonder
how often I truly feed the beast.

time there was,
when I was lean and lank;
the world was a jungle then.
to survive, one needed to be a tank.

then, the world mellowed with my age...
or, perhaps, it was myself which gave up the fight.
things no longer seemed so serious;
there were colors in between,
not merely black or white.

life was no longer a survival course;
living became an end, not a means.
harmony and happiness came from within;
struggle became as foolish as it seems.

the sun, once let in,
warmed, lightened and enlightened my soul;
night was merely a respite,
and love to all became my goal.

thus, sit I a-pondering...
I strive to give no ill.
I flow like water where I am led,
and God will take me where he will.

poem chain 1/29/13

A Line or Two for Ash Wednesday and Valentine's Day

who knew?
am I so old?
is my mind slipping cogs?
in the greater scheme of things
how interrelated it all is.
today is Ash Wednesday, the first day of Lent
ashes on the forehead of all the faithful,
ashes from last year's palms.
a time of sacrifice
and the forty days
leading to Easter and the resurrection.
Mardi Gras, Fat Tuesday
the true day of excess is past
gotta know excess to know deprivation, right?
coincidentally, tomorrow is also
Valentine's Day
Is it always that way?
I never made a connection...
is there is one?
bear with me
the Feast of St. Valentine was to honor
any number of St. Valentines
for various religious reasons...
I especially like Valentinus
who married Roman soldiers who
were forbidden to marry...
he also ministered to Christians, another no-no.
it wasn't until 1382 that Chaucer,
love those romantic Brits -
remember Henry the VIII?

put the romance, the hearts, flowers,
birds mating and cupids
into the mix.
whatever, whomever, the day thrived,
the day we celebrate the love
for our chosen partner -
human love, itself,
the excesses and the deprivations.
or... perhaps,
it does belong in the time of lent, after all.
celebrating, merely and purely, "love",
God's true gift to man...

  2/13-14/13

Writing

often, the words fall like snow
a flowing sheet of understanding
touching, cleansing, covering up
iniquities and foibles, misunderstandings and sorrows
renewing by the grace of God

other times, words come from the mouths of characters
babes and spirits, animal and human
a vignette, a tale, spun in such a way
that one may understand what
the word had to say

perhaps, an epiphany
causes a veritable waterfall of words
cascading madly through my mind and hands
until even I am overwhelmed
and spent

the word may come from a note
music wafting in the ether
swirling into images of time and place
or an image to the eye
unfolds itself into a who, why and what

God grant me the serenity
the perspicuity, the patience
to see, to record
to pass on to all the brethren
the gifts that thou has unfolded

2/26/13

Growing Up...

father
I was not a very good son
too much was expected
the high iron keep
which was my father
was a welcome security
against the uncertainties of life
yet the rooms were bare and stark
devoid of warmth
I could not long gaze
into those piercing, rending, eyes
without turning away
I was uncomfortable and alone

mother
she was a warmth unto herself
full of life and love
bringing a serenity to the chaos
of my father's order
it was she who nurtured
who taught and accepted
respected and understood
she was a barrier
between myself and
a world which I could not accept
which would have driven me away
if not outright destroyed me

son
I have been touched by greatness
by an exciting and ever-changing world
full of wonder and of grace
it was my parents who allowed me
to be a part of this
my father being the window
my mother the steady hand
willing to let go when the time was right
my father was the very image of all that was dark,
mechanical, fearful, lost and not understood
my mother's grace softened the blows,
the frustration of never being able to quite succeed

dogs
perhaps, the greatest gift my parents gave me
was the world of spirit
of unshirking companions, giving wholly,
of unceasing and undemanding love
a realm parallel to, yet far beyond,
the slippery slope of human endeavor
where no answers are needed
for there are no questions
here is life, success beyond measure,
kindred spirits with which to soar.
a plain in which I travel yet,
where I gain joy and knowledge

and on...
the mistakes of youth were made.
I can only say I loved
poorly, completely, devoutly;
I was touched by so many
and, I pray, returned such in kind.
I remember few male friends

who died or took very different paths
leaving a dark and painful hole within me.
it was the females who lighted my life
with them, there seemed to be no grudges, no pain.
once, I used to think that I was abandoned
and, in turn, I had abandoned others

until I realized
we are all intertwined,
a tapestry of trying our best,
of loving and of faith
we can only do what we must do
at any given moment
we are the sum of our past and our present.
'abandon' is a red-flag word like 'should',
with no meaning other than to give us guilt.
all who have ever touched me still reside within.
the words, music and images which I share
I pray I pass along in the same spirt
with which they have been given

for myself, I have been truly blessed

    3/12/13

Thelma Mitchell

Thelma personified three words for me

Texas -
she was a spirited and free soul
eager to understand, to learn.
her thirst was unbound
and her soul as giving,
as pervasive, as the wild wind.

Good -
always caring, nurturing,
going out of her way, without seeming to,
to reach others, to touch, to be touched
and help in any way she was able.
she left a warmth in the hearts of those she met.

Mother -
simply, she was...
to her three sons
to her church
to any and all who came
within her sphere.
one never felt alone or ignored
or uncared for
within her provenance.

Thelma was a gentle force, living and breathing,
lighting and taming the unbridled darkness of fear,
which follows too closely around us all.
her faith did not allow her to succumb,

nor did she allow others to.
the music which rides the wide open spaces
was echoed within her soul.
truly, she was a woman to ride the river with.

    3/18/13(7:35 am)

Interlude

I have been asked
why I so often write about the newly passed

I write about people who
have touched my heart,
leaving a thread of themselves
woven within me,
as I pray I may do for others,
for we are all intertwined
within this tapestry we call life.
I write to celebrate their life
I write to celebrate their transition
I write because it is what I am able to do

2013

Trusty Warriors

The automobile was white,
A mechanical monstrosity,
With a cow-catcher grill,
That would scoop snow up onto the hood.
The road could be seen flying by
Beneath rusty holes, not completely
Covered by sliding mats.
She was low-geared and her rear-end
Tended to clank while shifting.
Slow and steady, time and again,
She plodded through the mountains,
Finally dying in a vacant lot,
Her heart torn out and bequeathed
To a blue pickup truck.
A dirty blue, pickup truck,
With two hearts now,
Beating in harmony,
Hopeful tomorrow will be better.
As the night falls,
So does the orange skins,
Life fleeting, eroding away,
The memories stand steadfast.
Oh the memories,
Of road trips, hard work on farms,
Tears, sweat, blood, shed as they
Traveled, experiences shared,
A part of and chariot to a human existence.
Knowing as the last flake of metal
Rots away, the past is rooted in tales,

Shared to family and friends, of
The owners of these trusted warriors.

Doug Hodges & D. Everett Newell - 4/17/2013

Previously published in <u>Dinosaurs Live Among Us</u>,
D. Everett Newell, Rochak Publishing 2013
Printed with permission.

Wednesday Morning

I, as one of God's creatures,
am truly blessed
and give Thee thanks this new morning!
whether Ye be called Great Spirit,
God, Jehovah, Allah,
or any of innumerable names,
I believe in Thee!

I believe in God
and He believes in me
I am a child of God
I hear HIm...
in the rhythm of the wind
through the songs of the surf
in the laughter of rushing water.
and, He hears me...
when I sing in the morning
when I give praises
when I record the words He has given me
through His Spirit Animal messengers
when I listen and try to follow the path He has given to me,
my mind, heart, and action will follow.
all *is* right with the world
and in harmony
when I let it be

the rub, for me, is Man,
who, collectively, can not come to God
withoutbooks and rules
without power and control.

words may be inspired
and help us along our way.
I believe this is why I am given such,
why all scripture has been given.
just as I believe each living creature finds its own way to God,
God allows each living creature to find the way He has
provided
... and, most people seem to live this...
yet, they worship in clusters
following this pattern or that.
still, I am not bothered,
unless I, or anyone, is attacked
for being crazy
for being in league with the devil
for worshiping differently
for not following the "correct" interpretation of the Bible.
this disunity, in a message preaching harmony,
is ironic.

someone spoke of the rich tapestry of culture
how much each can offer the other
the amazing gifts each area is given by God
which can be shared
this includes not only food, dress, language, music
but faith as well.
there is a reason God appears where and how he does.
It is not for me to question or even understand the ways
of God.
unfortunately, I have met too many people only too happy to
do that.
I am merely here to love and help and worship and flow as
best I can,
in the way He has given me...
to be in harmony as much as possible
to humbly go where I am led

to follow scripture
to follow His whispers
to follow the universe as it unfolds...

I, as one of God's creatures,
am truly blessed
and give Thee thanks this new morning!

4/10/13

"They are new every morning"

- *Lamentations 3:23*

this next chapter in life
is obscured, not as clear
as in the past.
too many deaths have clouded my vision,
my mind too muddled with unfamiliar memories.
the sun is opaque, lost in a twisting sky,
I awake and... is it the sun? or, perhaps,
a fading moon at dawn?
without landmarks,
there are no directions.

for all that, this
creaking body arises each morn,
giving thanks and grateful for the new day.
time passing means merely more transition;
old things pass away,
new find their way into my existence...
it has ever been thus.
perhaps, in the past, I was less aware...
perhaps, the loss never seemed as great...
I refer, of course, to writing.

to stories, which no longer seem to flow
from a spirituality that lies within,
no longer without...*song left me a while back.*
I am still a wordsmith; communication still my passion
yet, like in the years with the newspapers,
words again have to be crafted,

molded, and presented.
they dance within my palm like the head of a cane
ready to be used... however... whenever.
the ether is but full of old rejoicings
I slide along the edge of a sharpened blade,
dreading to remain,
dreading to fall to either side.

rather, I ignore the predicament, altogether
and seek solace in the sky and in the earth,
in the comforts that I have known and loved.
I hesitate to embrace whatever change may be coming
yet, embrace it, I must
and in my heart and soul, I know this.
faith must be restored and onward I must march.

4/29/13

Three In The Morning

Happy

happy first day of the rest of your lives!
the world did not end... again
thanks be to God
Peace to all of us
as we go forward in love

12/21/12

Morning song

I used to wake to the virgin snow
and though I knew it was an illusion
I felt it washed away the iniquities of the world
and if, perchance, I saw an elk
then, I had no doubt

1/24/13

High country morning

there is frost on the branches
the saddle creaks with the cold
yet my body is warm from the coffee
my pony seems raring to go
the rising sun fills my spirit with joy
promising heat in the coming day
I laugh and watch my breath
drift away like the wispy dreams of night
I rub the pony's ear and slap him on the neck
we ride into the new day

my thanks, Dennis, for the remembrance- 2/30/13

Soldiers

New Day

Gettysburg - 150 Anniversary

'A brand new day!' was exclaimed
birds gathered among the branches to sing in the morning
the scent of coolness on the wind,
grass and tree in the air,
perhaps, even a cow could be heard lowing...

yet, there were other scents, other sights
like the row upon row of broken and bloody bodies
which stretched across the field and over the low stone wall
the occasional low moaning of some wretched soul
who the medical corp has missed
    among the mass of dead flesh

the arduous job of bringing wagons into the tangle of bone
of calming the skittish horses
of trying not to see, to breath the cloying air of death
of filling mass graves with the refuse of war
quickly liming and burying and going away

it only took three days to destroy an American crop of youth
to insure one future by taking away so many others
such is the way of war, victory and time
proving any wisdom and truth which may be gleaned
... it was long ago

now, the green rolls out before
dotted with statues and monuments
names and dates, less we forget the price of struggle
the heroes of both contesting sides, now ghosts
    gently wafting in the breeze
glimpsed among the trees, and out of the sun

Poem Chain, Summer 2013

Jenny

on the peripheral of your mind
you know there is a great war.
you know that tens of thousands
of soldiers now trod the dusty roads
you have walked every day of your life.
that the thick forests where
you played hide and seek, picnicked, and hid from boys,
are now torn with cannon ball and musket fire
a thousand bodies crashing and fighting
leaving the trees scorched, blackened and bloody.

yet, the everyday day to day is still your lot.
every day must be normal, more or less the same,
you gather wood, you heat up water,
you prepare meals, you prepare clothes,
you wash and wear your life.
as always, moving from duty to duty
trying not to think about what transpires beyond,
though the blood of your twenty years is excited
and the smell of gunpowder on the breeze
quickens your pulse.
still, the lot of your life is a ritual of one step at a time
despite the turbulent times.
how else does one survive
be brave and not go crazy with zeal
or break down into a quivering mass of despair.

you visit your sister and young child on Baltimore Street
for her husband is away
you knead bread dough in the kitchen,

perhaps humming some hymn
or newly heard marching tune.
you hear the sounds of war getting closer;
its current comes and sweeps around
the cabin like it was a rock
in the midst of a creek.
suddenly, you are hit,
a shot through the kitchen door,
and you die with a sigh
thinking that today was not
going to be the same as any other

> *Gettysburg, the 3rd day, July 3, 1863*
> *Jenny Wade, the only civilian killed during the battle*

personal note: I have spelled her name 'Jenny'; general consensus spells it 'Jennie'. Her given name was Mary Virginia. I have seen literature with both spellings. However, it was as 'Jenny' the poem came to me.

Doug Hodges 2013

Sunday

the congregation prayed for the woman
in the air conditioned church
on the flats alongside the Rio Grande
they prayed for strength, for guidance
for perseverance, for...

and Coyote was running, running,
as fast as he could down the trail through the brush
then, suddenly, before him
a gigantic chasm loomed
the grand canyon
with mountain high walls
infinitely far away on the other side
and the down, down,
down to a barely glimpsed thread of green
he turned on a dime
vertigo yanking at him
yet, without missing a beat
madly ran on along side of the great void
on and on as fast as he could go
the edge of the world beneath his feet
pulling at him as he sped

6/2/13

Don't go near the book -
You might want to go in

moving incredibly fast over the ocean
on a Nantucket Sleigh-ride
each wave hitting like a sledgehammer as on and on we go
tied by life and foam and blood and water and salt to the
largest creature of this earth as it truly runs for its life...
or lazing down the Mississippi on a hand-built raft
just me and my friends, Huckleberry and Jim
it's still a race; the slavers are hot on our heels
yet, the slow meandering of the great river
the warmth of the muddy water and the sun
lull one into realizing that what will come will come
when it does...
being pushed around by a one-legged father figure
yet, being taught and loved as never before
I find myself in an adventure of danger, daring deeds and
searching for treasure...
and, has it come to that?
could a human race of achievers truly allow themselves
to become mere fatted cattle for an evil race of predators?
... are we really thousands of leagues
beneath the ocean's surface
breathing in a mechanical beast,
more powerful and wonderful
than any surface vessel ever imagined?
... would we really chain a man to a tree to die
a horrible death
rather than shoot him? which would be more humane?
we shoot the dog? what would we do today?
... and how would we react, stranded on a deserted island,

left on our own to survive? what social structure
would we create?
would we create a social structure?
would chaos reign because of one
or for lack of one?

... history, time, adventure, romance, lessons and rhythms
are to be found for those seeking
reading, like singing and playing music, is a part of one's soul
one is immersed so completely, reborn with each new book
each new tale renews the spirit, energizes the mind
even from the dreaded non-fiction volume can be gleaned
pearls of wisdom and of light
all the words becoming a part of the you
who trod forth into your own world, armed and renewed
with the experience and test of those,
real and imagined, who have gone before

  6/18/13

Enjoying moments

enjoying moments should not be difficult
each moment should come in its own time
slowly, to be savored and fulfilled,
processed and integrated.
however, more often than not
moments come in waves
like the sea upon the shore
in a crashing crescendo
of built-up energy colliding with
a wall of anticipation...
a burst of activity,
of flashing time and poignant emotion,
of overwhelmed senses
finally climaxing in a great purge of self
... leaving but a pause
while heart and mind return to
a calming rhythm,
the world returns to normal focus,
breath comes easy and with clarity
and, we await the next
moment

poem chain 7/11/13

Promise Shining

a shining, slow time of peace,
that is the promise;
the hope and the goal.
God has given His word,
we must but understand.

we live in a world of chaos.
it has been so since 'the fall';
nations war with each other,
morality has stumbled and fallen,
man looks not to God for guidance.
he looks only to himself.

whether Great Spirit, Jehovah, Allah,
or merely called God,
harmony and love and true peace
are there, given for us but to see
and accept.
in His world, His universe,
as well as in numerous scriptures,
regardless of creed,
this is a self-evident promise.

His word is out there.
His word speaks not of violence.
it speaks, rather, of justice and harmony.
it speaks not of judgment,
as much as of consequence.
we are the sowers and will reap
as we have sown,
individually and collectively.

I speak not so much of bibles and selected scripture
but of all that God has spoken to us
since the beginning;
to the Jews, the Hindus, the Buddhists,
Native Americans, Native Africans, Celts.
on and on for God has spoken and does speak
to all men.
I speak not of religions, sects, cults,
organizations large and small,
who spiritually guide us on our way.

I speak of individuals, of animals,
of all of God's creatures,
placed upon this ship, Earth;
to be fruitful,
to be happy,
to be the personification of God...
of love, life and freedom,
living in harmony and grace.

ah, yet, does that demon freedom tempt us
into the sin (is that really a word or a lack of word)
of power, of greed and lust.
having fallen once, must man fall again and again?
seemingly so...
yet...
nature goes on.
the sun, moon, the stars,
birth and growth and death.
these do not stop for 'sin',
nor do they stop for man.
it is a wheel set in motion upon which
we may ride well,
or ride not so well.
our choice.

poem chain 8/12/13

Journaling

I journal solutions,
personal and esoteric solutions.
not only do I journal
how I may budget dwindling finances
or in what manner I fill
or unfill my home with furniture,
I journal the whys and wherefores
of the rain, of flooding,
of drought and fires,
of why I see certain people doing certain things,
or when or how often.
I journal of the birds and wildlife
of friends and family
the pets and children, thereof.
I journal of love, of God
the past and the great beyond.
for whereas my mind may be the great computer
of my existence,
my heart, the very purpose of that existence,
journaling is the bridge between
and it is therein, where lies my soul.

poem chain 8/30/13

Palo Alto, Texas - May 8, 1846

Palo Alto

if there were
    lessons learned,
they were lost amidst
    the shot and shell.
if there were
    lessons to be learned,
only Raven knew
    flying above the carnage.
war, as always, was merely
    endurance, survival and death.

10/4/99

Afterword

Perhaps, it is an old story now, especially to fans and reoccurring readers... for me, it can never be. It is my origin, my "Ah ha!" moment, the epiphany which changed my life and set me on my present road...

It is also the path and roots from which I came; times tumultuous, light and dark, which, like all of us, brought me to those crucial moments and decisions that make me who I am today.

I was born in the hills of Southern Bavaria, a tiny town called Herrsching-An-Amersee, in the country of Germany... was raised on the plains and in the mountains of Colorado, with a few formative years in Ottawa, Canada (hence, my love for the sport of hockey and british spelling).

By 1998, I had achieved virtually all I could ever have imagined... of course, not in exactly the form or manner I may have chosen... but I was successful, happy and content...

Not so content that I didn't recognize a need to do something... be something... something was missing and I didn't know what.

So, I went on a Quest to the Big Bend country of Texas where Raven (in form and Spirit) came to me and told me to stop... stop thinking, stop doing... stop racing my mind, my soul...

He suggested that I quit my job, sell what I owned, and go on the road... that as I traveled, he and other Spirit Animals would guide me... I would be taught and guided; I would hear and see the amazement of the world. I would be one with the currents of the air and earth and water... I would become a part of a world I only had imagined, even the world of my own self.

Man has taught himself to be superficial; his progress has left the soul and magic of the world, and very existence, behind.

I was surprised, everyone I know was surprised, that I took Raven up on the offer. However, in hindsight, how could I have refused?

The rest is an ongoing and reoccurring, never-ceasing journey that I have been blessed to travel. I have been honored and humbled by the gifts I have been given and I try, in these volumes, and with my songs, and by any communication to share what I have seen and heard.

My previous volumes are... <u>The Voice of Coyote</u>, <u>The Way It Was</u>, <u>Realms</u>, <u>New Vistas</u>, <u>Passages</u>, and <u>Alliances</u>... collections of stories. I also have two previous volumes of collected poetry, <u>Beloved Mystery</u> and <u>Flock of Dogs</u>.

These words reveal what has been given to me... words and rhythms to pass on, to share... tales, songs, images... the spinning of words and worlds, faith and spirituality, past and present and future, woven into a tapestry which, I pray, is enlightening, thought-provoking and, most of all, entertaining.

If you have been entertained, piqued, made thoughtful, or even smiled, with the reading of this book, then it has been a success. I have been blessed and I humbly thank you.

Feedback is always welcome and appreciated at *dhmoving2@ aol.com*.

Doug Hodges

Rio Grand Valley, Texas
July 2013

*I am honored to have been a member in the
CambridgeWho's Who Registry of Executives,
Professionals and Entrepreneurs since 2007.
http://cambridgewhoswho.com*

The most any Author can hope for, is imparting part of themselves with their words.... The most any of us, the readers, hope for, is an escape from the moment... When this happens, true magic is made... Leaving the trappings of an everyday, busy life, Doug (Hodges) is on a life quest. A quest, thankfully, he now shares with us. Like the majority of people, he is a work unfinished; what sets him apart, he knows this... Doug's words... move us. They pave a path to walk to their collective many new plains. Here we can think and compare our thoughts to his, as we look deeper into ourselves. This is the beauty of Doug's works; it is his and now, our gift!... If you have not read Doug's work yet, what are you waiting for!

- The Author D Everett Newell 4/08/2013